What people are sa

Adding To Your Finan

"...so simple it's actually enjoyable...investing really is for everyone..." ..." Manny Carbahal, CPA, Davis, CA

Building Your Financial Portfolio On $25 A Month (Or Less)

"...truly makes investing enjoyable..." Patty Lydon, Bookkeeper, Atlanta, GA

"...inspiring..." Pamela Hull, Financial Manager, Los Angeles, CA

"...a good solid book for novice...makes a lot of sense..." Patrick McKay, Sr., Postal Worker, Independence, MO

Getting Your Dream Life: Career, Sex & Leisure

"...positive, powerful and packed with good ideas for success in life <u>and</u> in business..." Barbara A. Scott, President, Zenar Books, CA

Getting A Free Education: The Key To Your Career

"...clearly written, delightfully easy to read...practical and attainable advice..." Sacramento Public Library

BUILDING YOUR FINANCIAL PORTFOLIO ON $25 A MONTH (OR LESS)

B. R. Christensen
E. S. Christensen

EFFECTIVE LIVING PUBLISHING
P. O. Box 232233
Sacramento, CA 95823

Published by Effective Living Publishing
P. O. Box 232233, Sacramento, CA 95823

Cover design by Tamara L. Dever, TLC Graphics, Orangevale, CA

This publication is designed to provide accurate and authoritative information in regard to the subject matter covered. It is sold with the understanding that the publisher is not engaged in rendering legal, accounting, or other professional service. If legal advice or other expert assistance is required, the services of a competent professional person should be sought.

Library of Congress Catalog Card Number: 96-091018

ISBN: 0-9643699-6-6

TABLE OF CONTENTS

INTRODUCTION

Welcome to the world of investing! We say welcome because this book is meant for the beginning investor or the person who wants to find a safe, secure place to put their money, where it will grow 100% or more a year, but without having to spend a lot of time doing the research or worrying about their investments. You will also learn very important information on how to cut out stock broker fees and expenses thus keeping that money in your own pocket. We feel it is important for everyone to take charge of their own lives and their own finances rather than put $1,000 of your hard-earned money into an over-diversified mutual fund that will grow no more than 30% a year and at considerable risk.

You will find all of the necessary steps, carefully outlined and in detail, to find these safe companies as well as how to actually do the investing. We feel everyone in this country should have access to this important information without having to pay hundreds of dollars for books, tapes, or seminars. We are not brokers and have no vested interest in any company mentioned in this book. Our purpose is strictly to educate. We are retired bankers and financial managers who have successfully used this method of investing for ourselves over the last 20 years as well as taught it to thousands of others

Afterall, we all know we need to save, both for our own well-being and for the well-being of our country's economy. Too often, however, we are lead to believe that we need to be rich (or at least have $1,000) in order to invest our money. No you don't! To make this information available to everyone, this book is specifically written to be easily understood by anyone from 13 years old to 90. After you have started your investment plan, share this with your children and grandchildren or, if you are a teacher, with your students.

The point of this book is to show you how to use just $25 (or less) a month to build your portfolio. But remember, $25 is a random amount we have chosen; you can use this same method of investing using less money or a great deal more. Keep in mind that this book is for people who want to invest SAFELY but with tremendous GROWTH. Because you will be using a safe method, fluctuations in the stock market will not effect your investment and you will be able to sleep nights without worrying.

This book is also for the person who does not find numbers or the stock market all that interesting and, thus, does not want to spend a lot of time on research. It takes a lot of time to invest in high-risk stock because you have to be constantly watching the market and making buying and selling decisions. With low-risk long-term investments, you make your decision choosing only from the safe investments and do not have to look at it again until you need to retrieve some money. If you find this book very interesting and would like to learn more about investing, see our flyer at the end on the sequel to this book, *Adding To Your Financial Portfolio.*

Please note that this is the 2nd edition of this book. The 1st edition of *Building Your Financial Portfolio On $25 A Month (Or Less)* won the 1998 Best Business Book of the Year Award and became a best-seller. Therefore, very little has been changed in this edition other than updating the figures used and changing some phrases for easier understanding.

Many people have helped with this book and supported our endeavors. Among them are Manny Carbohol, CPA; Bess Chen, Loren Kammerer and the whole staff of the Martin Luther King Branch Library who helped with the research; Bob Scott, a friend who understands mathematics formulas better than we do; Barbara Scott for her unflagging encouragement; our many seminar participants who showed us what they want and need to know; and our patient and self-reliant children, Anna and David. And to all of you who will, by using this information, help us fulfill our obligation to make a difference in this world.

Please use this method to build your own financial security and remember to have fun watching your money grow.

Bobbie & Eric Christensen
Sacramento, CA
October 1998

I. WHO CAN INVEST IN WHAT; AND WHEN, WHY, AND HOW SHOULD I INVEST?

Why Should I Invest My Paycheck When I Can Barely Make Ends Meet?

We all should! And that means anyone from 10 years old to 65 or even older. We have all heard this a thousand times. Even if our parents did not tell us, we would have heard it on a newscast or some talk show. So we all know how important it is to save for the future, but how many of us are actually doing something about it? How many are just procrastinating and then one day, or more specifically on our 60th birthday, realize we have put it off for too long.

And what is the major reason for putting off saving, besides procrastination? It is the same reason we put off most things in life - - money. We tell ourselves that we just do not have anything extra to invest right now, but we will some day. Some day has come!

Recently some of our schools have started teaching our children about investing for the future. Some (unfortunately not many) students in this country, from high school through college, have had fun playing investment games where they pretend to pick and buy stocks and then watch what happens. In the standard classroom setting, students are given $100,000 (just pretend money) to invest in the stock market. This is an excellent educational tool to help teach our children about one aspect of our economy. Wouldn't it be even more fun to use real money to teach your children how to invest safely? Obviously, we are not going to give them $100,000, nor should we. The problem with the method being used in our schools is that it teaches our children that the only way you can invest in the market is if you already have a great deal of money sitting around. Just recently on our local news, a school using this program was highlighted. The interesting thing about this news segment was that, after taking this program, most of the students said that when they were out of school and had a high paying job, they would invest in the stock market. Only two students understood that they could invest without having a huge amount of money.

By giving anyonc this much money in order to learn about the market, you are telling them that they **must** have this much money in order to be able to invest. This is just simply not true. However, if your intention is to discourage them from ever investing in their own future, you will do an excellent job of it.

What we should be teaching students, and everyone else in this country, is that the stock market is an opportunity we are all given no matter how much, or little, money you have. If a teenager is working and earning some money each week, they should follow the directions given here and watch their own money grow. And, if they do **not** follow these directions for **safely** investing their money but decide instead to choose risky investments, they will learn quickly why that is not a good idea and yet only risk loosing $100 or less. We think nothing of putting checks we are given at our babies birth into a savings account for them. Afterall, we want to save for our baby's future. But why not put it into an investment that will be safe and yet will have a great deal more growth potential.

The same is true for adults. It is safe to say that most people do not understand how the stock market works and, therefore, have developed the opinion that only the very rich segment of our population can earn "free" money in the stock market as well as other investment areas. We hear of someone buying $100,000 worth of stock and having it become $1,000,000 seemingly overnight. But, the majority of our populace does not have $100,000 to invest. The majority do not even have the $1,000 minimum necessary to invest in a mutual fund. Certainly not when they are in the twenties and just starting out in life. Yet this is the time that they should be saving for their first home or for retirement. After all, the government starts taking social security out of our pay checks immediately, so why shouldn't we take something out for our own financial future?

Of course, a regular savings account is an investment and you can put in just pennies if you want to, but it can be terribly boring watching your $10 grow by $.02 a month. With our investment plan you can watch it grow up to 100% a year or even much more, plus have the excitement of seeing a 3 for 1 split triple your investment "overnight". We will even show how an initial investment of just one share of stock and $25 a month can become $100,000. With our method you will be doing a little bit more than putting money into a savings acount but earning a lot more.

Some people have said that investing in the stock market, whether on your own or through an investment club or by way of mutual funds, is a legalized form of betting. Or perhaps you had parents like mine that taught you that everything in life is a gamble. You are gambling when you start a new job, get married, buy a house, and at many other times in your life. But we do not think of it as gambling because we feel we are investing in our future. When we marry, we know there is the possibility (and a very great possibility today) that it will not work out. Yet most of us will take that risk. Certainly one of the biggest risks we can take with our financial security is starting our own business, but thousands of people are doing just that every year, now more than ever. Most people, even kids, find a certain pride in having their lemonade stand, selling their extra produce, having a part-time consulting business, opening a computer training center, or any of the thousands of other choices in life. Having a small part-time business usually does not pose any threat to your financial well-being. But renting space, leasing equipment, hiring help, and opening a computer training center could be a threat.

Investing your money should actually be much safer then starting your own business. Yet the majority of new small businesses fail within the first five years. Why? Because they had not researched the market enough, they did not know how to market themselves, they did not have enough financial backing, etc., etc. When you invest in the stock market, you are investing in a company and becoming a part owner of it. Therefore, you need to do the same things you would do in starting your own business. That is, you need to research and find out if they know how to market themselves, if they have financial backing, if they are succeeding. In this book, we are going to explain how to do this research using just a few minutes of your time and, who knows, maybe you will learn things that will help you start your own successful business.

There is always the possibility of losing money when you invest it. However, by following our method, you will create minimum risk for your money with maximum gain!

Learning about the financial world and enjoying the excitement of this legal form of gambling are only very small parts of why you should be investing. The important reason for doing this is for YOU. Are there things you want in life but feel you will never be able to afford? Are you worried about your future and how you will survive when you retire? Are you in the majority of working people who cannot afford life insurance and, therefore, worry about your family if something should happen to you? Do you just want more out of your life?

Probably most people think at one time or another of owning their own business and, for one reason or another, never get around to doing it. Investing in the stock market is investing in a company and becoming part owner of it. You may feel that you do not have enough money to start your own business, but you have enough to invest in another business and take pride in watching that company grow and prosper and taking you right along with it.

What Can I Do With Only $25 A Month?

How about buy your first home or a new, larger home? Or get a college degree? Or even be able to retire early? If you are trying to save for your first home, you may be wondering whether owning a house is worth it if you have to save for twenty years just to get a minimum down payment. That in itself is a major problem because the smaller your down payment, the higher your monthly payment will be which will put even more stress on your small budget. Also, in today's market place, we all need to wonder whether investing in our own house is a good investment or will the value decrease below it's purchase price as has been happening in many areas of the country. But it does seem to be a natural instinct to want a place of our own. So do you think it would help if you could save all of the down payment you will need in 5 years instead of 10 years?

When you are in your twenties, you probably do not want to be tied down to a house and its payments, yet that is a good time to be saving for it. You might be reading this right now and saying to yourself, "I'm only 21 years old and plan on enjoying my freedom for quite awhile before settling down with a spouse, kids, and a house!" But even at 21 you can probably think of other things you would like to do. How about that trip around the world before you settle down or that Porsche. Or how about retiring at an early age.

The point is, you can and should invest in your future even if you do not have a clear goal. But it is certainly a lot more difficult when you do not have a goal. It is a fact that it is almost impossible to accomplish anything in life if you have not already figured out what it is you want. So if you have to, just invent something in your mind that you want to save for. After all, there is no law against changing your mind in the future when you have enough money from your investments to do whatever you want to do. But it is important in anything, whether career, family life, or your personal life, to have goals you are headed toward. If you need help with figuring out "what you want to be when you grow up", try reading my first book, *Getting A Free Education: The Key To Your Dream Job.*

If you are in your thirties, do you want to go back to school or do you want to help your children go to college some day? You can actually start your children on saving the day they are born with just a few dollars a month in the stock market. Then when he or she is old enough to work part-time, they can be adding to that every month. The same goes for your own education. Just because you cannot afford to go to college directly out of high school does not mean life is over. You can still have a wonderful career or start your own business, you can still marry and raise a wonderful and happy family without college. But if you start saving from every paycheck as soon as you get out of high school, you will be surprised at how quickly those few dollars can grow.

Do you want to live comfortably when you retire and/or be able to retire before age 65? That is probably the number one financial concern of people in their forties and upward. We know that the social security system was created as something to help the older citizen survive retirement. It is important to remember that it was never meant to be the sole support of anyone. Therefore, it is up to each of us to take care of our own futures. Currently, 4.5% of your pay check goes into the social security system. If you make only $5 an hour, that is about $9 a week or $36 a month. Could you afford to save that much each month for your own use? Can you afford to save just 1% or $8 a month?

You see, it does not take much to invest in yourself and, when you make your own investments, you are controlling it and do not have to worry about politicians using your money for something else or about it going bankrupt and you loosing all of your money. Then, if social security is still around when you retire, it will be what it was meant to be: an additional help in your retirement years, not your sole support. Let your government-controlled social security grow little by little but have your own investments grow 100% or more a year.

The point is, investing is a way to save for short term as well as long term things while remembering that short term investing is riskier with more of a chance of losing money (we will discuss this fully in chapter IV). A pension plan is a long term investment because it is meant only for your retirement with a sizable penalty if you withdraw **your** money early. And remember that even with a pension plan, we are talking about **your** money, not someone else's. When we talk about saving using our method for long term things such as a downpayment on a home, we are talking about 10 years (give or take a couple of years). That may sound like a very long time to you but, compared to a pension plan, it is very short time.

Social scientists say we are living in a time when people have come to expect "instant gratification". Well, those social scientists know that there is no such thing as instant gratification - - everything takes time. You and I know that, too. However, even after we lecture you on not expecting instant gratification, it is very satisfying to have your own savings system in place whereby you can watch your money growing on a monthly basis and know that you are the one doing it. It may not be instant, but it is filled with gratification. And you will have only yourself to praise for doing it and, believe it or not, you can actually have fun saving. After all, if you have a hobby of collecting something, say Christmas tree ornaments, it is fun seeing a new one added to your collection. Seeing your money increase in an easy and painless fashion can be just as satisfying. Maybe we should get rid of the word "saving" and instead call it "collecting"!

Should you invest to get rich? "The man who starts out simply with the idea of getting rich won't succeed; you must have a larger ambition." (John D. Rockefeller) The idea of Scrooge hoarding his pence is funny to us, but that is what happens when we invest just to become rich. Investing for your future is a much better ambition. And we would be willing to bet that if we asked you what you would like to do when you retire if money were no object, you could probably come up with some very interesting pursuits, and not one of those pursuits would be sitting all alone in a vault counting your money.

There was an interesting story we once heard about a typical couple who retired. He had worked hard at a blue-collar job all of his life. His wife had stayed home to raise the children and take care of their home. They had to pinch pennies, but they were happy. Then, when he retired at 65, his wife told him they had won a contest and the prize was a beautiful cruise to Hawaii. They had a wonderful trip, but he was spending a great deal of time worrying about how they would survive now that he was retired. She finally told him that he did not have to worry any more, that they had not won the cruise, but that she had been saving just a few dollars each week out of the grocery money and investing it in the stock market. Now they were quite wealthy and he would not have to worry any more. Needless to say, he was very surprised but very happy.

Unlike some of the infomercials you see on TV, we are not talking about getting rich. We are talking about putting your money into secure investments that will provide you with a comfortable living realizing that "comfortable" can mean different things to different people. We are talking about security for your hard earned pay check. However, likewise, we cannot promise that you will not become rich. For some people, having investments worth $100,000 is rich while to others nothing short of a billion dollars is rich. Also, becoming "comfortable" or "rich" depends on whether you follow our method so as not to lose the money you have saved and whether you follow our steps and thus increase your savings each month. It also depends on when you actually *start* investing.

We realize that it is easier to the read this book and say you are going to do it then it is to actually start doing it. If you begin saving when you are 50 years old, you will not be able to build up quite as much as you would if you started at 30. Likewise, by starting as teenagers at 13 years old, they will not only be assured of having a comfortable retirement but, in all probability, will be able to retire at a much younger age.

What we can promise you is that our method provides a safe way to increase your savings at a much faster rate than your savings account or mutual fund ever will.

Where Can I Invest My Money Safely?

There are many investments to choose from including stocks, bonds, Certificates of Deposit, treasury notes, real estate, mutual funds, and others. But this book is devoted to investing SAFELY but with much better growth then any of these other vehicles can provide. In chapter IV, we will be talking about all of these choices and each of their pros and cons, but our method uses only one possible investment. And what do we consider a safe place to put our money?

The stock market. The stock market?! Safe?! Are you kidding?! No, we are not kidding. Before we get into a brief description of all of the other options, let's see why the stock market can provide you with the best return in the safest manner so you will have something to compare the others to.

First, keep in mind that the stock market has out-performed all of the other forms of investment since the turn of the century (yes, including the crash of 1929). Since 1929, the stock market has increased in value 3 out of every 5 years. Unfortunately, due to the inability of others to invest wisely, too many people feel that the stock market is gambling. It is not gambling if you are investing in safe companies to begin with. Our purpose is not to give you a complete history lesson here, however, if you would like to see the actual research showing that the stock market outperforms the other investments, *Stocks For The Long Run* by Jeremy J. Siegel is excellent.

Second, remember that there are steps to follow in order to invest safely that we will be covering later. If you decide not to follow these steps and start investing in riskier stocks with the hope of a faster growth, you will be risking your own future. If you are looking to become rich overnight and invest in those stocks that have a vague chance of increasing dramatically in an extremely short time period, you are risking losing your money dramatically and extremely quickly. And the risk of that happening if you do not follow this method is extremely high. Historically, the individual investor who sticks with safe investments has always made more money then stock brokers have.

The third reason to invest in the stock market is that it is the one we can all afford. As the title of this books says, you can invest $25 or less every month and then sit back and watch your investment grow. You might think that joining a mutual fund or an investing club is the same thing but it is not. These both require a good deal more than $25 to start with (usually $1,000) without the safety or huge growth.

The fourth reason is actually a number of good reasons: the stock market allows you to choose your own investments thus giving you complete control of your money, you can actually become part owner of a company, and it is fun.

Many people have said that investing in the stock market is legalized gambling. If you are already addicted to gambling, do not get into the market until you get medical help. Gambling addiction is a compulsive illness that can be overcome. To invest wisely, you MUST invest with your head, not your heart. Occasionally you can invest using both your head and your heart, but not very often. The co-author of this book once decided, against the advice of her husband and co-author, to invest a few dollars in a new company started by a famous actor that she was very fond of. She purchased 10 shares at $17 the day this new company went public on the stock exchange. This stock has never seen $17 since that day. Fortunately, she didn't lose much but she now understands about using your head rather than your heart when you invest in anything. However, we will now contradict ourselves.

Occasionally you can invest using your head AND your heart as when we invested in Disney. Its long term history is excellent (so our heads were satisfied) even if we did spend our honeymoon at Disney World (our hearts told us to do it). Actually, this demonstrates one of the best reasons for investing in any company and that is **invest in companies that you know and understand and use**. Besides being very familiar with the Disney movies, we knew their parks (we visit every year), how they are kept neat and clean, the great attitude of their employees, etc. If we had gone to a park and found it dirty and in disrepair, we doubt that our hearts would have said "this is the one".

In the following chapters, you will learn how to develop your own investment plan that will give you a road map to carefully follow and to keep your emotions in check. Just like a road map, if you do not follow your financial plan, it will take you longer and cost you more to get where you want to go, if you get there at all. Developing a plan probably sounds very much like getting organized. Well, it is necessary to become at least a little organized. For some of you, that means "oh no, I can't do this, I'm totally unorganized". Don't panic. We have written our method down in book form and in detail just to help you. You will have all the steps carefully numbered so you won't forget anything

Besides giving you the details of what to invest in and how to invest, we will be helping you with other areas directly connected to your financial plan. To develop your plan, you will need to decide how much you can invest and where to invest it. Also, if you learn here how to **write down** your plans, you will find that having everything in black and white will keep you from making serious mistakes. In fact, if you can learn to create written plans to continually read and follow, you will avoid making mistakes in all areas of your life.

Remember also that if you keep in mind that you are investing for the long term or what you will have after 5, 10, 20, or 30 years, you will be less likely to make mistakes caused by greed or fear. Greed can lead you to make investment purchases trying to become instantly rich and fear can make you sell a safe investment and, thus, lose future earnings you would have had. We all must take chances in life, but we must learn how to take carefully researched chances that we know, in all probability, will succeed.

You may work for someone else right now but, when it comes to investing your money, you are working for yourself and you are the boss. As such, you must learn not to make decisions based on your fear of what the market might do tomorrow (no one can truly predict this). It is not actually "fear" anyway. What most people feel that keeps them from accomplishing so much in their lives is a small nagging doubt. People who are constantly buying and selling are either trying a false way of getting rich quick (that is to buy low and sell high over and over again) or they are letting their doubts and emotions make their decisions. As we have already pointed out, if you are investing in safe companies, your stock will quickly regain whatever you might have lost during a brief downturn or even during a longer recession if you hold on to it and don't panic. Do not waste your time watching the stock market every day trying to decide if you should sell this stock and buy that stock. Relax and enjoy the cozy feeling of knowing that your money is safe.

Certainly you can buy stock when it costs the least amount and sell it when it is at it's highest amount but that is what we cover in our book for intermediate investors, *Adding To Your Financial Portfolio*, who want to spend time every day on their portfolio. The point we are trying to make is that you can be investing a little each month in a safe company and still be following the rule "buy low and sell high". We will explain that later. Buying and selling every day is not fun and will just keep you from getting a good night's sleep.

We will be investing in stocks considered to be in the blue-chip category, that is, in large, healthy, growing companies that will still be around when your grandchildren are investing. Please do not confuse OUR blue-chip list with the blue chip list the New York Stock Exchange considers "blue chip". It takes the market a long time, sometimes years, to catch up with what is actually happening in the stock market. Therefore, stocks that are extremely stable can take years or even decades to become an actual Blue Chip Stock even though they have already reached that status in the real world. You will be developing your own list of blue chip stocks based on your own sound yet easy research.

Always remember that when you buy stock in a business, you are buying a part of that company. So, do you want to buy a get-rich-quick dream or a solid American business? Yes, we have all heard of the entrepreneurs who buy into a small company and then one year later sell their stock at a profit to "get rich". You have to decide for yourself what kind of person you are. Do you really want to gamble your whole future everyday on such a risky investment? Psychologists tell us that security is an ingrown need after food and shelter. Therefore, we are assuming in this book that the vast majority of people want security. We personally want security for our own money. Thus, our method of investing is based on safety for our money and yours.

Generally speaking, the smaller the company is, the riskier the stock is. Also, any stock that sells at $10.00 or less is usually remarkably risky. Historically, the odds are extremely high that company will not make it.

You may have wished that you had invested in some of the technology stocks when they first came out but, when they first became public, no one had any way of knowing which ones would succeed and which ones would fail. And the vast majority of the technology stocks have not done well even though we remember only the ones that have changed the world, so to speak. Remember that it does no good to worry about the one that got away. You will do best to think about what the future of that successful technology firm will be. Right now it would seem that MicroSoft can do no wrong, but what about 10 years from now. There was a time when Apple Computer could do no wrong but things changed. If there is a world-wide catastrophe such as a financial collapse or even natural disasters, will technology be considered a basic necessity of life? When natural or man-made disasters occur, we know that people are concerned with rebuilding their homes, finding grocery stores that are open and have food and water to buy. After a hurricane, flood, tornado, etc., schools are concerned with rebuilding and getting the basic supplies, not buying new computers. A business that has been physically ruined will be back in business quickly if they supply a necessity of life rather than the unnecessary things. We will be discussing the difference between the necessities of life that people will always need and the other things in life that come and go depending on the situation later in this book.

It is always fun to play the "what if I had invested in MicroSoft the first day it was issued" game. But that is a very chancy game to play with real money. Doesn't this just prove that the stock market is too risky? Not at all. We will be showing you how to find the success stories that you will not have to worry about. And we are not bashing MicroSoft but only pointing out something that all technology companies already know or should know. That is, until the day arrives that we literally cannot survive, live and not die, without technology, it is not truly necessary. So long as we can shelter ourselves and grow food and find clean water without technology, it is not necessary. But it certainly does make life a lot easier and more pleasant! Remember that we have invested in Disney stock and that is certainly not a necessity of life. We will be talking more about investing in the necessary stocks first and the unnecessary ones as our portfolio grows.

Remember that one of our primary goals is to invest our money where it will grow to give us more wealth. According to numbers compiled in 1994, the Standard & Poor 500 has shown a 9% return during the last 25 years, out-performing corporate bonds (4.4%), treasury bills (3.3%), and inflation (3.3%). Of course, the stock market has drops that can effect the day to day value of your portfolio but, in the last 50 years, the safe secure stocks that have dropped have regained their original value in no more than 42 months. That means that to invest safely in the market, you must invest for the long haul so that you will not have to worry about how a recession or brief drop is affecting your portfolio. Plus, you actually save money by not constantly buying and selling.

The obvious savings is in knowing that stock brokers charge for every purchase and sale (or transaction) and, even using our method, you may be paying a one-time broker fee for an initial purchase or subsequent sale. Therefore, you want to be very sure that the stock you are holding is going to drop in price and continue to drop before you decide to sell it and, using our method, you should end up with stocks so strong that their value will always rise again.

Remember that one of our points is to make investing fun and something you do not need to be an expert in. If you have to watch your portfolio every day to decide whether to buy or sell, you will not be having fun. Of course, there are those people who do consider that fun, but we are writing for the average citizen, just like us, who considers traveling, snorkeling, hiking, going to the theater and such as a lot more fun. Our method is only for the person who does not want to become an expert in investing.

It is a fact that many ordinary citizens have consistently made better market decisions then the professional analysts and brokers have. In 1995 the book *The Beardstown Ladies' Common-Sense Investment Guide* became a best seller because this group of older women had a higher rate of return on their investments than any stock broker in the country (not including the unnecessary broker fees and expenses they paid). After all, even the best educated analysts and brokers are just people and they do make mistakes. Then, to double their mistakes, they insist on buying and selling continually. If you feel you must deal with these people, NEVER follow their advice without first checking the stock yourself using our step-by-step method in chapter IV. Many years ago, the co-author worked for a large stock brokerage firm in Boston. It seemed amazing to her at the time that, even when the broker invested unwisely and a person lost not only what dividends had been earned but even lost their initial investment, that person still had to pay the broker's fee every month. In other words, the broker makes his money whether he makes a good decision for you or not. Please consider that brokers only make that fee when they buy or sell a stock for you; thus, you will find that the stocks in any one mutual fund will be continually changing.

If you think that you need a Ph.D. in order to invest your own money, let me ask you how many rich Ph.D.'s do you know? Besides, as Ben Franklin the creator of the first public library knew, you can learn anything you want or need to know at your library. In fact, virtually all of the research we will be talking about can be done for free at the library. Even if you find yourself enjoying the complexities of the stock market and want to become an expert in it, you can get all the advice and knowledge of the very best experts from the books those experts have written at your library. You never need to depend on just your local broker's opinion.

For that matter, do not completely depend on and trust anyone else's opinion. You would be amazed at how many of your friends and relatives will be more then willing to offer their advice on investing your money. You should certainly listen to these people and gather all the information you can but, as you listen, you must consider whether they actually know what they are talking about. You may have a sister who works as a bank teller, but that does not make her an expert on banking; however, you need to consider whether she has done extensive research on the banking industry and what outside places she is getting her facts from. In all probability, if she is repeating what her boss has told her concerning how safe an investment in her bank is, you are hearing the morale boosters that all of the employees hear. But if she is quoting The Wall Street Journal and other ethical business magazines, you may want to follow up her research with your own to see if this particular bank is a good investment.

It is not necessary to be an expert with a complicated system to succeed in the stock market. You will find that our method is very simple and takes very little time. You can spend as little as a couple of hours a month on your investing or, if you find it more interesting than you thought it would be, you can spend lots of time on it. Stock brokers are considered experts in the field but there are not many rich ones; if they are rich, why do they still work so hard to get your fees? And the stock market itself is not that complicated to understand. If you want to start a company and need cash to buy a building and supplies, then you look for investors. Once you have that business established and want to expand your company, you again look for investors. That is what the stock market is. The system of buying and selling on the floor of the New York Stock Exchange is very confusing, almost seeming to verge on mayhem. But only a brokerage firm that has bought a seat on the floor of the stock exchange can be on that floor so you do not need to worry about all of that mayhem. However, if you are going to be in New York, the stock exchange does give very interesting tours.

Nevertheless, it is a certain fact that no one is more interested in your money then you are! Well, with the possible exception of Uncle Sam and, as you get older, your children. You have worked hard to earn your money and you should be the one making decisions on how to invest your money. Trusting someone else to do what is best for you is never a good idea and definitely not a good idea when it comes to your future survival and comfort.

To answer the original question, what should you invest in order to have safe low-cost investments that you will not have to constantly watch and become an expert in? **You are going to learn how to find the large, well-known, growing companies and then how to save money while using every technique available**

to increase your investment quickly and safely.

Everyone Who Has Played "Monopoly" Knows It Takes Money To Make Money; Can I Be Successful Without A Big Bankroll?

As William J. O'Neil said, "Success in a free country is simple. Get a job, get an education, and learn to save and invest wisely." Hopefully, you already have the job (if not, order "Getting A Free Education: The Key To Your Dream Job" by this author on the form at the end of this book). And everyone should be constantly learning new things. This book will give you the knowledge you need to save your money and invest wisely.

O'Neil also said that in his experience "a person's years and quality of education have very little to do with making big money investing in the market." And he is right - - even children can learn to invest and some of the most successful investors in history never graduated from high school. However, he left out another very important point. It also does not matter whether you are a man or a woman. When it comes to investing our own money, we are all created equal and there is no "glass ceiling" on your potential. Women can invest as wisely as men and you do not need your spouse's permission to invest your own money. And guess what? The opportunities in investing are equal for everyone, regardless of race, religion, or age, too! Our country is supposed to be a free-market society and, when it comes to investing, it really is.

And finally, if you do not ever take the first step toward securing your financial future, you will never reach it. As we always say, if you don't believe you can, then you can't. We know that getting past the little doubts and taking that first step in any endeavor is always the most difficult one, but we hope that this book will give you an easy plan to follow and will reduce the fears you may have. Only you can take those few dollars to make your first investment. Even if you never invest another dollar, at least you will have done something for your future. But we certainly hope that you will continue to invest. We know that you can do it.

II. WHAT TO INVEST IN!

So What Can I AFFORD To Invest In?

Let's talk about some of the different kinds of investments and the pros and cons of each. For each one we will need to keep in mind certain factors such as how much money is required to get started, how safe is it, how fast will it grow. We are only considering some of the most common savings methods so that you can easily compare these systems with the stock market. Knowing that at this point you do not want to use all of your spare time working on your investments, we are not considering the many other savings options that require in-depth knowledge, huge fees, large initial investments, etc. Keep in mind the four reasons we listed for investing in the stock market: **it has outperformed all other forms of investment, it can be very safe if done properly, it is within even a very tight budget, and it allows you to control exactly what happens to your money.** Compare the history of security, ease of use, and the amount of initial investment needed for each of the following with that of the stock market.

Savings Account

For those who are younger in our reading audience, there used to be a time when putting your money into a savings account was an excellent investment. When we were children, we never received lower than a 5% return on our savings and sometimes as much as 10%. Now our banks are very profitable to their Boards of Directors but not to the public whose money they use to create that profitability for their owners. Currently, you can only expect about 3% and be prepared to have service charges taken out of your account also. Therefore, you might want to consider investing in the banking industry but don't think of a savings account as a way to secure your future.

Also, keep in mind that with several investment instruments such as savings accounts and Certificates of Deposit, you are actually giving your money to someone to invest in the stock market for you. The difference is that you put your money into a regular savings account and get 3% interest on your money. At the same time, the bank is using your money to invest in several things along with the stock market and getting as much as a 15% or more return and giving you only 3%. The banks attitude is that they are giving you the privilege of investing with them so that they can give you as little as possible and they can make as high a profit as possible. Instead, why not develop your own attitude of investing where you will get the highest return for your money and always remembering that you are giving the bank the privilege of using your money.

However, having said all of this, we confess that we will be using savings accounts in our method, but in a very limited way. After all, everything has its proper place.

Certificates of Deposit

We don't think Certificates of Deposit should be called CD's any more due to the possibility of being confused with something that goes into our computer. But for the brevity of this book, they will be called CD's.

A CD is money that you choose to invest in a type of savings account that, because of the high initial investment and the fact that you cannot touch your money for a guaranteed amount of time, will give you a higher rate of return. Many banks have a minimum deposit of $1,000 or more along with a penalty for early withdrawal. If you have this much extra money sitting around that you can tie up for at least one year, then you might want to look into a CD after carefully checking all of the possible interest rates. They vary widely. This is certainly a very safe place to invest your money. However, we are interested in investments that require a much smaller initial sum of money and will actually have a higher rate of growth.

Real Estate, Gold, and Collectibles

Real estate can be very lucrative, but you can also quite literally lose your shirt in it. Whether or not real estate is a good investment is very dependent on the economic situation of the country and even the specific area of the country you are interested in at the time, and that situation can change very quickly. With today's housing market, even owning your own home is not necessarily as good an investment as it used to be. Nationwide recessions have taught us that the value of the house you buy can easily drop below what you paid for it and it can take as long as 10 years to get that value back, if ever.

Of course, the value of any investment, including the stock market, can also change very quickly. However, our major concern is that real estate is not "liquid". That is, if the real estate you have invested in does not seem to be doing well and you want to get out of it, it can take a very long time to sell your property. Other investments can be sold as quickly as making a phone call. Therefore, even if you are aware that the value of your house or even the apartment building you bought is dropping, it is not always feasible to quickly sell such property. And while you are waiting for a buyer, you will be watching the value continue to drop. Also, even considering what you might hear on a late-night infomercial on TV, it is safe to say that it takes a little bit more than $25 a month to invest in real estate.

We consider gold and collectibles as one category with real estate because they are physical items that one collects. You buy up real estate expecting to either make a quick profit by selling it again at a higher price or make a small profit each month through rental. You buy gold and other collectibles with either the thought of making a long-term profit or just for the fun of it. People can collect anything of gold to see what it will be worth in the future the same as they can a Renoir painting or even Barbie dolls. Any kind of collecting of items should be done with the understanding that you are doing it for the enjoyment of owning these things and fully understanding that it may never, at least in your life time, increase in value. With this in mind, remember that we want to invest our money to see actual real growth in a safe manner.

Mutual Funds

A mutual fund is a collection of different stocks and other investment types that you buy along with a group of other people. The idea is that by going in with other people, you can all afford to jump into investing in a bigger way and also meet their minimum investment requirements. Some mutual funds are discussed under Pension Plans (see below). Mutual funds were created by brokers who realized that they could make a great deal more money in fees and expenses if they only took on clients who would invest at least $1,000. If they have 40 people investing a minimum of $1,000 in a month, they make more money than if they have 40 people investing only $100 in a month. In other words, dealing with the small investor was not worth their time and effort because they were looking for a very large income from other people's money.

However, it has been interesting to watch as the initial amount has been dropped over the past two years. In fact, now there are brokerages, though very few, who will take as little as $500 for an initial investment. Will this amount go lower? We do not know but it seems to be going in the other direction. Fewer and fewer brokers are willing to do the one share transaction.

With some mutual funds, you have a limited amount of control over which companies (or types of companies) you will be investing in and, in others, you have no control. The mutual fund buying and selling will be controlled by your broker to a greater or lesser extent. Again, you must answer the question of whether you want someone else making the decisions concerning your money and whether you are willing to spend a very small amount of time to handle your finances yourself in order to have control of the situation as well as save on the fees. You can find mutual funds with excellent track records considering that excellent means up to 30% growth a year. But what will their track record be next year? If their record declines, you will need to be ready to make a change. The broker handling your investments may be excellent, but what will happen if there is a personnel change? Again, you will need to make a change.

Mutual Funds can give you more diversity in your investments more quickly in that you would have shares in over a hundred different companies. However, for this diversity you are: (1) paying a management fee even when your investment loses value; (2) facing personnel changes that may make better or worse decisions for you; and (3) risking your money on a huge portfolio with some very risky stock involved that you have no choice over. Of course, for our purposes, the major problem (4) is that a minimum investment of at least $1,000 is usually necessary. At $25 a month it will take you over 3 years to save enough to start investing and that 3 years can be very discouraging. Recently, some mutual fund businesses have lowered their minimum investment to as little as $500 a month, but this is contingent on investing $500 every month, no matter what your situation. These high initial costs are why so many investment clubs have sprung up. Obviously, a group of people pooling their assets can meet the minimum dollar requirement and afford to jump into a mutual fund quickly (see below).

Investing in one of the hundreds of Mutual Funds available takes a lot more research than the average person usually wants to do. To intelligently invest in a Mutual Fund, you need to fully understand front-end loaded funds (admission fee of as high as 8% plus the usual management fee), back-end loaded funds (up to 8% fee when you sell plus the usual management fee), closed-end funds (you buy at a discount when it is offered but cannot sell unless they allow it and you still pay the management fee), and many other terms which seem to be increasing monthly. All of these different funds were created to make you think that you are getting a good deal ("Gee, I don't have to pay a fee until I sell when I can afford that 8% fee because all of my investments will have gone up!"). If you do not understand them, you can end up losing a great deal more than you put in originally.

Investment Clubs

Investment clubs have become quite famous in this decade thanks to the Beardstown Ladies, a group of older women from the town of Beardstown, Illionois, some retired and some not, who formed a group to learn more about investing and to pool their money in order to meet the minimum investment (usually $1,000) required by brokers. They became famous because they were able to choose stocks and investments in which their return was much higher than the Standard & Poor 500 (S&P 500), a cumulative index of the best rated stocks on the market. Perhaps the major reason that our public thought this feat was worth a book about the Beardstown ladies is that it seemed amazing to some segments of our population that anyone, including women (and in this case, even elderly women) can learn how to build their financial portfolio and take care of their own money. We do not find this at all amazing. Anyone, regardless of race, sex, religion, or age, can learn to take care of their own finances very easily. The secret is that one word in the previous sentence, "learn". If you are not willing to learn, then you cannot do it. Knowledge gives you power, therefore, you should continually be learning new things, including how to increase your financial worth. Besides, isn't it fun watching your investments grow?

What do we dislike about a club? Do you really want to trust your money to other people? These co-authors own four businesses between the two of them; and yet, he has no partial ownership in her businesses and she has no partial ownership in his businesses. Why? Because too many good friendships (and marriages) have broken up due to joint business ventures. In a club situation, everyone votes on which investments to participate in and you must go along with the majority vote. How many of you are working for a boss who is making the wrong decisions for the company and there is nothing you can do about it? Do you want to get into that same kind of situation? When you are investing your own money, it is the same as having your own business. Therefore, you can and should make your own decisions. For some people, a club makes it easier to sit back and let others make decisions for you and thus, we suppose, to have someone else to blame for any mistakes made. However, we have found that clubs are having a problem with members dropping out because they do not like doing the calculations involved every month. If you are in a club having a problem with drop-outs, consider letting your math-fearing members use our method of research so as not to scare them away just because of numbers.

Aside from the question of who is controlling your money, most clubs go through regular brokers which will cost you more. Granted, they listen to the suggestions made by their brokers and, therefore, seem to be getting their money's worth. But you can do what a broker will do for you, and better than they will do it, on your own and for free. However, as we have said, the law requires that you deal with a broker and we, therefore, use only discount brokers in our method. The reasons for this will be explained shortly.

IRA's and Employee Pension Plans

The current maximum yearly amount you can put into your IRA (Individual Retirement Account) is up to $4,000 *per couple.* As this is a maximum, you can open one for much less. If your budget allows for this, we encourage you to do so. An IRA may not have the liquidity or the high growth of the stock market in that you will pay penalties for early withdrawal under age 59 1/2, but it is a guaranteed source of income for retirement. Be aware that you are still putting your money into a mutual fund.

You may work for a company that offers an employee pension plan such as a 401K plan. With this type of plan, you contribute a set amount from each pay check into a professionally managed fund. These plans allow you to defer or put off paying taxes in the year your money was earned while still earning interest on stock appreciation.

Sometimes the company also contributes a set amount. If you are working for such a company, we suggest that you take advantage of this program. Whenever your employer matches what you put into your pension plan, you should join it as their share is just free money in your pocket. However, always be aware of where the funds are being invested, i.e. stock market, mutual funds, etc. because then you need to read what we have said about each of those areas.

If your pension fund is being invested in the company you work for, you need to be particularly carefully and research how well the company is doing. We suggest you follow the method we outline in chapter IV. However, since you are working in that area already, you will have additional places to research. For instance, if you are working in the banking industry and have the opportunity to invest in your particular bank, you will want to contact the public relations department for a copy of their annual report, talk to a senior vice president about the outlook for the company, call any contacts you have at other banks to chat about the banking industry as a whole (are they being bought out, are they closing any branches, are they laying off personnel). This will give you more insight into your industry, but you will still want to follow our suggested research in chapter IV to get totally unbiased opinions also.

After all, you are probably emotionally involved in your employment to the point that you would put your own money into a company that is not necessarily a good investment, or not as good an investment as you could otherwise make. Research your employer carefully along with other stocks in the same industry and compare it to other types of industries to decide where your money will do the best for you. Any information you can collect is only useful if you can determine its validity by comparing it with other information sources.

Stocks

Investing in the stock market got quite a bit of bad press back in 1929. One huge crash (which initially only wiped out those who had invested borrowed money that they did not have and ended up bankrupt) and the word was out -- the stock market is too risky! And yet, our method is based almost entirely on the stock market. Why? Because it is where you have the **greatest potential** for the highest gains and, if you follow our advice and use your own intelligence, you should have **very safe investments**. We could suggest a method that would have the potential for huge fast gains but would not be safe, and this we cannot condone for the beginning investor. We feel that the public needs to know about the great opportunities available through our stock market. You have as much right to increase your wealth as anyone else even if you are starting from a smaller base. It is only our individual greed that says "it won't do me any good to invest just $25, it would take too long". Too long for what? Have you been given one month to live? It is **greed** speaking when you feel its not worth it because you will only have $100,000 when you retire instead of $1,000,000. It is **sensible** when you feel $100,000 is better than ending up with just social security (hopefully).

And learn from the past: **Invest only what you can afford to lose**, not everything you own including your first born! This is true of anything you invest in. After all, even banks have been known to close leaving their savings accounts to payout only a fraction of what their owners had put in. And too many small businesses have gone under because of trying to keep the company open after it had already stopped breathing! Finally, invest only what you can afford to lose, because we personally know that there are lots of things to enjoy in life right now. You do not want to scrimp and save every penny just for retirement. You have to enjoy life now also.

We will be investing in **common stock** instead of preferred stock for several reasons. A business will only issue a limited number of shares of preferred stock, there is no reinvestment plan for it, usually no dividends are paid, and it will have limited growth as compared with common stock.

The purpose of this book is to increase your capital. However, having lived and worked all over this world, we both feel very patriotic (we realize how old fashioned this sounds) about the United States. We firmly believe in the capitalistic system that gives us the right to start our own small businesses (90% of businesses in this country are five or fewer employees). As we both come from early pioneer stock, we also firmly believe in our lives only having a purpose if we are taking care of ourselves and then, with our success, helping the less fortunate. Thus, we would like to point out that when you invest your money to build your own capital, you are also helping the backbone of this country, private enterprise. When we are young and struggling, there seems to be nothing left to even help ourselves. Then, when we have learned a great deal more, we may not have a lot of money, but we have time to volunteer to help others. But eventually, through 90% hard work and 10% luck and intelligence, we have enough to share with others financially. So, help yourself and help your country and your neighbors by investing in the stock market and in American companies.

III. HOW TO SAVE MONEY

After Paying The Bills, How Can I Invest In Anything?

One of the main reasons people use for not investing is that they have nothing left after paying all the bills. There are obvious solutions to this such as taking on a part-time second job (the co-author once worked three jobs at one time, however, she was single at the time). But usually you do not need more money than you currently have to start investing.

An often overlooked fact is that stocks can sell for only a few dollars or over a hundred dollars per share. We are not talking about penny stocks that are here today and gone tomorrow. But the price of a share of stock, in even a huge company like Coca-Cola, can vary from $40 to $150 a share, give or take a few dollars. In the next chapter, we will talk about how to choose which stocks to invest in. For now, all you need to know is that you will need about $75 to get started. "Wait a minute!!! You said I only needed $25 or less a month to invest!!" Okay, so you need a little bit more to get started with and then you follow up with the $25 every month.

Our method is this: You only need to invest in one share of stock (let's say about $40 worth) to get started and then invest $25 a month (or less) which, along with reinvestment of dividends and splits, will keep your money growing.

Even using our method, it is still the law that a broker has to do the transaction for you but, using a discount broker (see below), the first minimal purchase of one share of stock at $40 should cost you about $35 in broker fees. After your initial investment, you no longer need to pay a broker, unless buying stock in an additional company. So to start with, let's concentrate on getting that $75 you need to get going.

1. How Much Per Month. On the cover of this book, it is clearly stated "on $25 a month (or less)". The methods we are going to be talking about can be used for any dollar amount whether you can afford $5 a month or $200 a month. Only you can decide how much that monthly dollar amount should be. The examples we will be using in this book are all based on $25 as that is an amount that just about anyone has available each month. However, if you are a student mowing lawns or a single parent working two jobs, you can still use these methods but at a lower monthly amount, even only $5 a month. You see, the rate or percent at which your money grows will be the same no matter how much you are contributing; it just may take a little longer to get where you want to go. But you will get there! If you invest in a strong, safe company that is showing its investors a 30% annual growth rate, you will get that 30% whether you are investing $25 a month or $200 a month. In other words, it may take you longer, but you are being treated exactly the same as everyone else.

It does not matter whether you are investing $5 a month or $200 a month. What is important is that you invest the same amount EVERY SINGLE MONTH! I can remember years ago setting up a Christmas Savings Account so I would have enough to buy presents for the holiday. But guess what? It seemed that each week (or month) I just did not have that $5 to put into the bank. Thus, the first (and only) rule of saving, which you have probably heard many times, is **pay yourself first**. No one else is going to take care of your finances, nor should they. Only you can save your own money.

You need to go over your budget and see how much you can afford to invest each month (not weekly) without going hungry. Go through your check book for the past few months and make a list of every bill you paid and every item you bought for each month. From this you can get an idea of what your regular monthly bills average as well as how much you tend to spend on extras. Then make up a typical monthly budget for your family showing the dollar amount you spend for rent/mortgage, groceries, gas, electricity, etc. Then write down what your paycheck is each month plus any other money that you get every month.

Hopefully, this list will show that you earn more than you spend. If not, then it is time to cut back wherever you can. Cut out the lunches and take a bag lunch, stop renting videos for awhile, make an effort to cut back on electricity usage, etc. In the end, you want to have a few dollars left over not for you (all of these bills every month are for you) but rather for your future. After all, if you just cut out one family meal at McDonald's each month, you would have saved enough money to get started. The end result from your list should be a dollar amount that you can afford to invest each month comfortably, even if it is only $5.

For ease in understanding, we will refer to $25 a month throughout this book even though you may have a different amount in mind. In order to use this method correctly and to **build** your financial portfolio, you must treat this $25 as a regular monthly bill, the same as you would your electric bill. You must have a specific day each month that you write yourself a check for $25 and put it into your savings account. Perhaps when you write out and mail the check for your electric bill, you could write and mail a check to your savings account. Or when you send in your monthly mortgage payment, send in your savings account payment. However, if you do have automatic payroll deposit where you work, you can save yourself the mental torture of parting with the $25 by having it automatically deposited into your savings account. Check with your payroll clerk. If this is not currently available, talk to your fellow employees and, if enough of them are interested, your company might decide to look into automatic deposit.

We told you this method does not take a lot of your time. Therefore, after you have started your investment plan, pick one day a year (we suggest on New Years Day), to go over your budget and see if you can increase this amount. If your family budget will not tolerate an increase, that's okay. And if an emergency comes up, its okay to cut your monthly amount back. HOWEVER, if you must cut back, do not tell yourself it will only be this once. Cut back to $10, or whatever you can **easily** save out each month, until you are sure you can safely increase to $25 again. And do not increase your monthly amount unless you are sure that, for the foreseeable future at least, you will be able to maintain that monthly amount. We want you to enjoy your investments so choose a monthly amount that will work well for you, not an amount that will bc too difficult for you. Just like in smoking a cigarette or having a drink at a certain time every day, being **consistent** is very important in creating your savings habit. If you get used to paying yourself each month, it will soon be a habit that you will not even think about. So pay yourself first.

2. Start a savings account. Yes, we told you a savings account is much too slow. But you need that first $75 (this is an approximate dollar amount) to get started, and we want to stay within our $25 a month budget. For some of you, sitting down and writing a check for $75 may be relatively easy. But if your budget will not stand that sudden jolt, put your monthly $25 into a bank savings account. After all, we are only talking about saving for three months to get the $75 you need to start with. Three months will give you plenty of time to do the research required in the next chapter. Even if you can only save $5 a month, it will take you only fifteen months to get started on your investment plan. And fifteen months is not long when you check our examples and see what the long term results will be. In fact, waiting and building that first initial investment can be as much fun as planning and waiting for your vacation - - half the fun in going on a great vacation is in the planning. Also, if you do have to take several months to get started investing, try writing down what you get for interest each month from your monthly bank statement. Then when you do start investing and getting quarterly reports, you can compare the figures with what your money was doing in your savings account and have a big smile on your face (smiling is a very healthy thing to do). Even most teenagers, if they are willing, can save $5 a month.

After you have actually made your first investment using your $75, you will continue to use this savings account. Depending on the company you choose to invest in, you may only be able to reinvest in your stock quarterly, but you will still need to save that $25 each and every month. So every single month, on your pay day, you need to go to the bank, write yourself a check, and put $25 into that savings account or send it in for more stock. We will talk later about how to actually do the reinvesting.

If the company you have invested in allows you to buy additional shares monthly, then by all means send that $25 check directly to them, with the appropriate paper work, every month. After all, there is no sense in letting the bank grow rich off of your money if you can be investing it yourself every month. Otherwise, let your money build up during the quarter and then reinvest it.

IV. THE METHOD

Now That I've Got A Little Stash, What Do I Do With It?

As soon as you put your first $25 into your new savings account, it is time to start THE METHOD. Basically, The Method is picking out **what** stock to invest in. Note that we said stock, not stocks. We all know the expression "don't put all your eggs in one basket", however, we also feel that one egg is better than no eggs! When should you **diversify**? Invest only in one company until you have 50 shares of it and then let it build on itself while you start investing your $25 a month in another company.

Why should you consider diversifying? Any economy is cyclical meaning that sometimes the economy is good and sometimes it is not so good. It also means that the economy as a whole can be doing fine, but a particular industry is not doing so well. You could decide to invest in an oil company realizing how important oil is for every day transportation as well as all of the synthetics we live off of. But it only takes one oil spill to drop the value of your investment overnight. In all probability, your stock will go back up again and continue to grow, but while it is down in value it is nice to have other investments that are still doing very well. The economy in a particular section of the country will also have its ups and downs. This can affect the value of some stock and it can affect your wallet. Finally, your own personal economics can be stronger at times and weaker at times depending on whether you are getting more overtime pay, develop a second source of income, lose your job, etc. Since all of these things can effect your investment plan and the price of your stock, it is a good idea to diversify. Then, if you suddenly need some money for a family emergency and must sell some stock to raise the money, chances are that at least one of your investments can be sold at a profit or sold for more than what you originally paid for it.

Please be wary of over-diversification which mutual funds do by buying into 150 or more companies. When investing in *safe* companies, we suggest owning stock in no more than 6 companies.

Which company should you start with? We want it to be safe to protect our savings but we want it to be growing so that we do not have to do all the work. If it doesn't grow, you might as well keep your money in the savings account or under your mattress!

To determine which stock is right for you, we need to do a little research. Don't panic! We said **a little**. You do not need to become an expert in the stock market to invest in it. And you do not need to spend a lot of time. You can spend two hours at the library and pick out your first stock or you can spend a week. But, again, this book is meant for people who do not find investing all that interesting (only the resulting increase in your money) and want to spend as little time as possible on this activity. There are two excellent resources, both available for free at your public library, that you will need to look at: Value Line's Investment Survey and The Wall Street Journal. Sounds pretty scary, doesn't it? Especially when you get to the library and find that the Value Line's Investment Survey is a huge book and each daily Wall Street Journal is the thickest newspaper you've ever seen! It's okay - - you are not going to read these, only use certain information in them. But before using either of them, you need to start with the first step.

1. Gut Instinct. "Gut instinct??!! How can I use gut instinct on something I know nothing about??!!" Don't underestimate yourself! You know the market place much better than you think you do. You probably know which stores to shop at to get the best bargains. And you probably know which brand to buy to get the results you want. Even teenagers know which video systems sell the best or which brand of clothes outsells all the others year in and year out. In fact, if you as an adult are considering these types of companies, you should get a teens opinion first. This is what we mean by gut instinct - - choosing things that you personally know about and have experience with.

Sit down with paper and pencil and start listing the things you really like using. What brand products do you always use because you feel they are the best on the market? What stores do you shop at because you feel they are the best? What is (or would be if you could afford it) your favorite vacation destination? What is your favorite car? Your favorite restaurant? Also, only look at the large companies as, historically, the stock of larger companies has always outperformed the small company stocks. If you feel good about a certain product or service, chances are that part of the reason is that it is large and well-known making other people also feel good about it.

Obviously, there are thousands of things you could put on your list so we are going to list them according to area to make our decision making more manageable and in order to be ready to diversify when the time is right. We feel that there are three areas of investing that cover the essentials of modern life: food/beverage, gas, and some pharmaceuticals. However, under thc non-essentials of life are: leisure, some manufacturing, service industries, automobiles, a new house.

The reason we make a distinction between essential and non-essential things is that the first group will always be necessary in our civilization. We must have food and drink and, in this age, our gas and electricity as well as fuel (for heating and to run the car) to just get by in today's civilization. That means that no matter what happens, short of a nuclear war, people will always buy these things. Even if there were to be a severe depression/recession, people still need food and drink, to keep warm and cook their food, and to get to any possible work to earn money. Certainly this is a worst case scenario, but it makes these companies the safest to invest in. Other industries, leisure, manufacturing and service industries, etc. would be the first to collapse during a major national or international problem. Even during a small recession with some people losing their jobs, the first things to be cut out of the family budget are vacations, that extra wide-screen TV, eating at restaurants, buying a new car or house, etc. Since economics will always be cyclical in our world, we concentrate on buying stock in the essential areas until we have our nest egg and then we can diversify into the non-essential companies.

So start with two columns on a piece of paper, one being essential and one being non-essential. Then list each of your products and services that you particularly like under one of those headings. It is a small organizing step that will be very useful when you are ready to diversify because diversifying means going into a completely different area. If you start by investing in a company in the food industry, you would want to diversify into another area such as utilities or shelter.

Having a cyclical economy is why we use older, well established, large companies like Coca-Cola and Disney as examples of what $25 a month can do for you. We are not recommending Coca-Cola or Disney but only giving you real examples of what your small investment can turn into. If you are trying to teach your children about investing and they seem a little uninterested, try showing them the examples we have created to show them how their small amount can grow without them having to do anything for it. Remember that you should never invest in any company, no matter what your "gut instinct" is or what your friends say or even your broker tells you, until you go to the library and do a little research.

2. **Research.** After you have listed all your preferred products and services, choose several of the ones you are personally familiar with and that are the most well-known to begin your research with. If you have the time and the inclination, you can certainly research every one of the companies on your list. But, again, we are assuming you do not want to spend lots of your spare time doing this.

When you get to the library, you are going to first use the Value Line's Investment Survey (this can be purchased but is very expensive or you can use it online but at an additional charge). Remember also that you can make copies at the library of the pages you want to study further. The reasons for the Value Line's importance are that everything you need to know about a certain company is on one page, including an 18 year history of highs and lows, and it is relatively easy to understand. If you do not easily understand some parts of it, do not worry as those parts are not as important anyway unless you are trying to make riskier investments in order to make a fast buck. Here is what you need to look for:

a. As in 1 above, look for companies you are familiar with and feel confident in. Then make sure they are large and well-known before continuing your research. It is always better to invest $100 in a good stock than to buy 50 shares of a $2 stock that has extremely little chance of helping your portfolio.

b. Remember, you want a stock with good value. Value stocks have always out-performed stocks that are growing too quickly (growth stocks). Osborne Computer developed the first lap top computer and was a fast growing stock, but it could not keep up with its competition and in three years was out of business even though it had tremendous potential and was, at the time, recommended more than Microsoft was. A growth stock has the *potential* to make you a lot of money but, unfortunately, the history of growth stocks proves that value stocks are much, much safer and *will* make you a lot of money. **A good value stock should show increasing earnings over the previous five years at least, preferably ten years.** We will explain later how to tell the difference between value and growth stocks and stocks that are both value and growth stocks.

c. Look for a company that is constantly expanding its market by creating new products or moving into other countries. A business cannot keep increasing profits if it is not growing. But it is important to keep in mind that growth can also be a bad thing. You will need to check out whether a company is trying to grow too quickly and is, therefore, headed for trouble, or if the company is having strong, normal growth. We will be talking about how and where to find this information.

d. If the top management of a company owns large percentages of stock in it, you can assume they would not invest their money in a problem company. Likewise, if you read or hear something about top management selling large blocks of stock, it is time to be very careful.

On the next page is a typical Value Line page. We are going to use Disney Corporation as an example of how useful Value Line is and what you need to look at and understand on each page of Value Line in order to make your decision as to which stock to start your portfolio with.

When you go to the library and ask the reference librarian for the Value Line, you will be handed a book about 4 inches thick. An edition is published once a week and added to the back of the book. Therefore, when looking for a specific company, just start at the back of the book and go through each section. Companies are listed alphabetically.

Please note that Disney would not be in one of the essential areas but will give you an interesting demonstration.

DISNEY (WALT) NYSE-DIS

RECENT PRICE	72	P/E RATIO	29.5 (Trailing: 32.4 / Median: 21.0)	RELATIVE P/E RATIO	1.83	DIV'D YLD	0.7%	VALUE LINE	1779

TIMELINESS (Relative Price Performance Next 12 Mos.) **4** Below Average

SAFETY (Scale: 1 Highest to 5 Lowest) **2** Above Average

BETA .95 (1.00 = Market)

1999-01 PROJECTIONS

	Price	Gain	Ann'l Total Return
High	120	(+65%)	14%
Low	90	(+25%)	7%

Insider Decisions

	J	F	M	A	M	J	J	A	S
to Buy	0	0	0	0	0	0	1	0	0
Options	1	0	1	1	0	0	1	1	1
to Sell	1	0	1	1	0	0	1	1	1

Institutional Decisions

	4Q'95	1Q'96	2Q'96
to Buy	355	534	375
to Sell	247	172	311
Hld's(000)	248157	314607	307135

	1985	1986	1987	1988	1989	1990	1991	1992	1993	1994	1995	1996
High:	7.3	13.7	20.6	17.1	34.1	34.1	32.4	45.3	47.9	48.6	64.3	73.0
Low:	3.7	7.0	10.3	13.5	16.2	21.5	23.4	28.5	36.0	37.8	45.0	53.3

Target Price Range: 1999 | 2000 | 2001

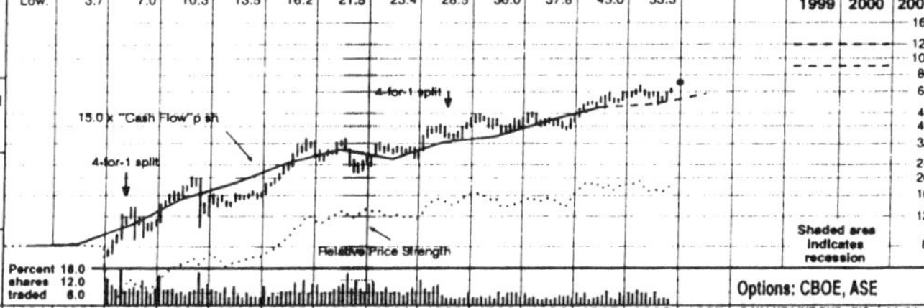

Options: CBOE, ASE

1980	1981	1982	1983	1984	1985	1986	1987	1988	1989	1990	1991	1992	1993	1994	1995	1996	1997	© VALUE LINE PUB., INC.	99-01
1.77	1.94	1.93	2.37	3.07	3.89	4.73	5.46	6.45	8.49	11.09	11.87	14.31	15.93	19.19	23.10	*31.10*	*35.85*	Revenues per sh [A]	*53.65*
.34	.31	.27	.33	.40	.55	.71	1.02	1.26	1.65	1.95	1.73	2.16	2.34	2.90	3.46	*3.60*	*4.15*	"Cash Flow" per sh	*7.00*
.26	.23	.19	.17	.19	.32	.46	.71	.95	1.28	1.50	1.20	1.52	1.63	2.04	2.53	*2.25*	*2.65*	Earnings per sh [B]	*4.85*
.05	.06	.08	.08	.08	.08	.08	.08	.10	.12	.14	.17	.20	.24	.29	.35	*.42*	*.50*	Div'ds Decl'd per sh [C]	*.80*
.31	.64	1.15	.60	.36	.36	.34	.53	1.12	1.39	1.36	1.78	1.04	1.48	1.96	1.71	*1.85*	*2.10*	Cap'l Spending per sh	*3.50*
2.08	2.25	2.39	2.54	2.14	2.29	2.71	3.50	4.43	5.62	6.62	7.43	8.97	9.39	10.51	12.68	*24.15*	*26.30*	Book Value per sh [D]	*37.45*
517.67	518.93	533.62	552.15	539.66	517.50	522.80	526.80	532.80	541.20	527.20	520.80	524.40	535.50	524.10	524.40	*682.00*	*683.00*	Common Shs Outst'g [E]	*684.00*
11.0	14.6	17.6	25.3	18.7	14.7	20.3	21.1	15.8	16.6	19.3	23.3	22.4	25.3	21.1	20.4	*26.9*		Avg Ann'l P/E Ratio	*21.5*
1.46	1.77	1.94	2.14	1.74	1.19	1.38	1.41	1.31	1.26	1.43	1.49	1.36	1.49	1.38	1.39	*1.70*		Relative P/E Ratio	*1.65*
1.6%	1.8%	2.3%	1.8%	2.1%	1.6%	.9%	.5%	.6%	.5%	.5%	.6%	.6%	.6%	.7%	.7%	.7%		Avg Ann'l Div'd Yield	*.8%*
						2470.9	2876.8	3438.2	4594.0	5844.0	6182.0	7504.0	8529.0	10055	12112	*21200*	*24500*	Revenues ($mill) [A]	*36700*
						25.4%	29.5%	27.3%	28.3%	25.5%	20.5%	21.4%	22.6%	22.0%	22.6%	*21.0%*	*21.0%*	Operating Margin	*21.0%*
						124.8	143.1	148.6	191.5	203.1	263.5	317.3	364.2	409.7	470.2	*910*	*1015*	Depreciation ($mill)	*1430*
						247.3	392.3	522.0	703.3	824.0	636.6	816.7	889.1	1110.4	1343.6	*1555*	*1830*	Net Profit ($mill)	*3350*
						46.5%	46.0%	38.0%	39.0%	37.8%	37.5%	37.3%	37.6%	34.8%	34.8%	*44.0%*	*44.0%*	Income Tax Rate	*44.0%*
						10.0%	13.6%	15.2%	15.3%	14.1%	10.3%	10.9%	10.4%	11.0%	11.1%	*7.3%*	*7.5%*	Net Profit Margin	*9.1%*
						481.8	774.0	990.7	980.9	1378.4	1323.3	1813.8	1690.8	1662.0	2294.0	*d900*	*d300*	Working Cap'l ($mill)	*d100*
						540.0	529.5	423.8	782.0	1560.1	2074.3	2020.4	2088.0	2773.8	2855.6	*7500*	*8000*	Long-Term Debt ($mill)	*10000*
						1418.7	1845.4	2359.3	3044.0	3488.6	3871.3	4704.6	5030.5	5508.3	6650.8	*16465*	*17950*	Net Worth ($mill)	*25600*
						13.6%	17.4%	19.5%	18.7%	16.7%	11.9%	13.0%	13.5%	14.4%	15.3%	*7.5%*	*8.0%*	% Earned Total Cap'l	*10.0%*
						17.4%	21.3%	22.1%	23.1%	23.6%	16.4%	17.4%	17.7%	20.2%	20.2%	*9.5%*	*10.0%*	% Earned Net Worth	*13.0%*
						14.5%	19.0%	20.0%	21.1%	21.5%	14.2%	15.1%	15.1%	17.4%	17.5%	*7.5%*	*8.5%*	% Retained to Com Eq	*11.0%*
						17%	11%	10%	9%	9%	14%	13%	14%	14%	13%	*19%*	*19%*	% All Div'ds to Net Prof	*17%*

CAPITAL STRUCTURE as of 6/30/96

Total Debt $11705 mill. **Due in 5 Yrs** $5810 mill.
LT Debt $7005 mill. **LT Interest** $390 mill.

(Total interest coverage: 4.5x) (30% of Cap'l)

Pension Liability None

Pfd Stock None

Common Stock 680,670,488 shs. (70% of Cap'l) **as of 7/15/96**

CURRENT POSITION ($MILL.)	1994	1995	6/30/96
Cash Assets	1510	1943	868
Receivables	1670	1792	3029
Inventory (Avg Cst)	1387	1730	4420
Current Assets	4567	5465	8317
Accts Payable	2475	2842	6503
Debt Due	163	129	4700
Other	267	200	--
Current Liab.	2905	3171	11203

ANNUAL RATES of change (per sh)	Past 10 Yrs.	Past 5 Yrs.	Est'd '93-'95 to '99-'01
Revenues	20.0%	17.5%	*18.5%*
"Cash Flow"	21.0%	12.5%	*16.0%*
Earnings	25.0%	10.5%	*15.5%*
Dividends	14.5%	20.0%	*18.0%*
Book Value	16.5%	14.5%	*22.0%*

Fiscal Year Ends	QUARTERLY REVENUES ($ mill.) [A] Dec.31	Mar.31	Jun.30	Sep.30	Full Fiscal Year
1993	2391	2026	1937	2175	8529
1994	2727	2276	2354	2698	10055
1995	3302	2923	2764	3123	12112
1996	5893	4986	5087	*5234*	*21200*
1997	*6750*	*5750*	*5850*	*6150*	*24500*

Fiscal Year Ends	EARNINGS PER SHARE [A, B] Dec.31	Mar.31	Jun.30	Sep.30	Full Fiscal Year
1993	.50	.39	.48	.26	1.63
1994	.68	.45	.49	.42	2.04
1995	.84	.59	.60	.50	2.53
1996	.83	.31	.59	*.52*	*2.25*
1997	*.91*	*.42*	*.70*	*.62*	*2.65*

Cal-endar	QUARTERLY DIVIDENDS PAID [C] Mar.31	Jun.30	Sep.30	Dec.31	Full Year
1992	.044	.053	.052	.052	.20
1993	.052	.062	.062	.062	.24
1994	.062	.075	.075	.075	.29
1995	.075	.09	.09	.09	.35
1996	.09	.11	.11	.11	

BUSINESS: The Walt Disney Company operates Disneyland, CA and Walt Disney World, FL (Magic Kingdom, Epcot Center, Disney-MGM Studios). Supplies entertainment for theaters, TV & video. Licenses rights; publishes books; records music. Sells via catalogs & Disney Stores. Owns The Disney Channel. In Feb.'96, acquired Capital Cities/ABC for cash & stock. Earns royalties from Tokyo Disneyland; owns 39% of Euro Disney SCA, France. Foreign sales: 19% of revenues. '95 deprec. rate: 5.1%. Employs 81,000; has 580,000 shrhldrs. Bass trust owns 6% of stock; Directors/Officers, 3% (11/95 proxy). Chairman & C.E.O.: M.D. Eisner. President: Michael Ovitz. Incorp.: Delaware. Address: 500 South Buena Vista St., Burbank, CA 91521-7320. Tel.: 818-560-1000.

Disney's long-term growth prospects have whetted investor interest. Shareholders who have bid the recent price to new highs are looking beyond some temporary difficulties in the television business. At least, ABC is not the only network finding it hard to cope with an exceedingly competitive TV environment. There is certainly competence enough in the Disney/ABC organization to work things out eventually. Despite the runup, these good-quality shares ought to appreciate in line with most stocks over the next 3 to 5 years. But they're not timely with respect to likely performance in the year ahead.

A number of impressive recreational projects are under development. Excellent recent results for the theme parks justify continuing investment in this area of special expertise. The 25th anniversary celebration will help boost attendance at Walt Disney World in the fiscal year that began October 1st. A $100 million, sports-themed attraction will be ready early in calendar 1997. The following year, Animal Kingdom, a fourth Disney theme park, will open at the Florida complex. The first Disney cruise ship will also be launched in 1998, with another soon to follow. Future plans also include a large convention center, to be named Coronado Springs.

Expansion will proceed as well at other promising locations. Work will commence in 1997 on Disney's California Adventure, a $1.4 billion theme park near Disneyland, planned for completion in 2001. Farther away, the company and its Japanese partner are considering an aquatic theme park venture near their successful Tokyo Disneyland venture.

The theatrical film and home video business has ample momentum. The holiday season is off and running with near-record opening box-office returns for *Ransom*. And estimates in the trade suggest blockbuster figures for the live-action remake of *101 Dalmations*, which is just now being released. Also, favorable reviews imply a good run for *The English Patient*. A further contribution to fiscal first-quarter results is due from some 21 million *Toy Story* videos that have been shipped to retailers. Making up for weakness at ABC, strong growth is continuing for ESPN and The Disney Channel.

Edmund B. Swort, CFA November 29, 1996

(A) Fiscal year ends Sept. 30th. Quarterly amounts adjusted to sum to annual figures. (B) Primary earnings. Excludes nonrecurring items: '84, d$0.02; '87, d$0.09; '93 d$1.08; '95, $0.07; '96 Q2, d$0.51. Next earnings report due mid-December. (C) Next dividend meeting about Jan. 27. Next ex-date about Jan. 8. Dividend payment dates: about Feb. 16, May 17, Aug. 16, Nov. 22. (D) Includes intangibles. At 6/30/96: $18.1 billion, $26.57/sh. (E) In millions, adjusted for stock splits.

Company's Financial Strength	A
Stock's Price Stability	70
Price Growth Persistence	95
Earnings Predictability	80

Do not be frightened by all that small print jammed into such a tiny space as we are only going to be using a few parts of this prodigious material. The rest of these facts are for brokers and consultants and people who want to spend a great deal more time on their investments and who usually are willing to take a lot more risk with their capital.

Probably the easiest place to start is the written description in the lower right corner. This is an unbiased expert's opinion. It is not actual fact as no one can predict the future, but it is the opinion of an expert who spends his whole life studying these areas (isn't it nice to get an expert's opinion for free). This description always includes how the stock is expected to perform in the future, what the company has been doing recently, and how these activities should affect the future of the stock. This is one area to read carefully.

In the upper left corner is an item called SAFETY and, for Disney, it is listed as "2 (above average)". A 1 or 2 is acceptable for us.

Below SAFETY is 2000-02 PROJECTIONS. One column is called Annual Total Return and is showing a high of 14% to a low of 7%. We are looking for safe stocks that should produce about a 9% Annual Total Return to at least equal the S&P 500 historical return. Keep in mind that **a 14.7% return means that your money will double every 5 years**. If we take the average of 7% and 14%, we get about a 10% return on Disney. So an initial investment of $25 would be worth about $47.50 after 10 years. Doesn't sound like much, does it? However, you would continue to invest $25 *every single month* (a total of $3000 out of your pocket), or $4650 in 10 years.

But this amount is still not the total you would have earned. You will note in the graph part that Disney had two 4 for 1 splits, each 7 years apart. Therefore, it is safe to assume that, in all probability, it will have another 4 for 1 split, or at least a 2 for 1 split, in another 7 years. And guess what? It did. It had a 3 for 1 split in 1998. That brings your monthly investment to a value of over $10,000 potentially. How's that for just $25! You will actually end up with much more because these types of strong companies have always out-performed what even the Value Line has predicted (see our Coca-Cola example).

The chart in the upper right corner of the Value Line page shows the history of the stock including splits and the increase in value. This is a good visualization of how the company has been doing. The other information can be very interesting but not necessarily important in making your decision. As with the companies annual report, you need to be somewhat skeptical of dollar amounts reported as the company will do what it can to make the figures "look good". Basically, **we want to know that**

this company has been increasing in value over the last 10 years (stable and safe) and has had good dividends and splits (your money grows without your effort). Of course, you may find yourself becoming more and more interested in these reports and wanting to read and understand more of this information which *Adding To Your Financial Portfolio* does.

Now that you know what you will be looking for, take your list of possible investments, go to the library and look at the Value Line page for each of the companies you listed above using step 1, Gut Instinct. While at the library, you will need to either take notes on what you see for each company or make a copy to take home and study and make your notes right on that page. You may find, while still at the library, that you know which two or three companies you would like to invest in or you may need to think about it a little more. Either way, your next step is to look at The Wall Street Journal. The Value Line is necessary to get the history and the opinion of what the future is for this particular company. The Wall Street Journal will let us know if something is coming up in the very near future that we should know about.

Yes, we are talking about THE Wall Street Journal that most of us think was created for only a specialized segment of our population that watches the stock market 24 hours a day! Relax, it is just another newspaper that happens to specialize in accurate and truthful business news. It is also very educational. Again, you might find yourself reading more and more of the financial news and enjoying it more, but do not be discouraged if at first you feel like you are reading a foreign language. If you find yourself exploring The Wall Street Journal in greater depth, you will discover that the articles usually explain things carefully and simply enough for most of us to understand, ***if*** you ***want*** to understand more about the business of the United States as well as the rest of the world. Be advised that some people who are very serious investors also invest in foreign markets. As we said earlier, sometimes our economy is down when another countries economy is heading upward. But, as recent history has shown us, foreign investing is very risky. We also have personal feelings about investing in foreign companies when we can be helping our own American companies.

And don't worry about how BIG The Wall Street Journal is. There are only two pages you will be looking at: (1) the front page and (2) the inside cover of Section B for the Index of Businesses. However, keep in mind that for some people the stock market is addictive and you could find yourself wanting to learn more. In that case, there is no better tool than The Wall Street Journal.

When you first start reading The Wall Street Journal, it may be as difficult as trying to understand a foreign language. But you can learn a great deal through osmosis. If you decide to subscribe to it and start reading it daily, you will slowly learn what is being said and what it means. It gives you today's unbiased investment, business and economic information as well as all the facts you need to do your own research in a more in-depth fashion. And if you feel more adventurous, it will benefit every citizen of this country to understand at least a little of how the business cycle operates in this country and why it operates. As much as the business cycle can be annoying when it effects our jobs and lives, it is what keeps this country the strongest in the world. If you are upset when the economy effects your job status, we suggest a socialist country where jobs are guaranteed.

The Wall Street Journal is the unbiased source you need. First, glance over the front page to look for any mention of the two or three companies you have tentatively picked out (the articles will name the company in bold print). Then look at the Index of Businesses usually located on page two of the B section. This index has all of the companies that have articles written about them in this issue listed alphabetically by company name so you can just scan for anything in the rest of the paper about your company and read those specific articles. Do not worry if during the past few weeks you see no mention of the companies you are considering. As they say, no news is good news.

You have already researched the history of the company up to the current time so no mention of it only means everything is continuing as usual. However, if you find articles talking about trouble, you need to pay attention. And if you find mention of an upcoming split, you REALLY need to pay attention.

While getting started, you will need to look at the last two weeks of this daily paper to see what has been going on. You might learn that your third choice is going to split next week making it necessary to decide whether to move that company up to your first choice or not. If your choice is now selling at $150 and is due to split on the first of next month, you would be wise to wait until the official split so that you can buy your stock at $50 a share (3 for 1 split). Or, in researching your choices, you could find out that the president of the company you had chosen sold off most of his holdings last week and you decide to choose your second pick instead and wait and see what happens with company number one. Again, your library will have the recent issues available. What kinds of information will you be looking for?

For instance, in the December 13, 1996 issue, we found the follow interesting information:

1. Michael Ovitz resigned as President of Disney recciving a severance payout of $90 million after only one year in office.

2. Bank America took a $280 million charge back and closed 120 branches, eliminating 3700 jobs.

3. Chrysler idled the Belvidere IL plant due to slow sales of the Neon.

What does this mean? It does not mean anything by itself, but it gives you questions to ask yourself. If the President of a company resigns after only one year with a large severance payout, you want to ask yourself who will become President and in what new direction might that person take the company that will effect your stock? If the company you have invested in is cutting back with eliminations, how will that effect the price of your stock (it could go down until things settle) and how will it affect your stock long term (cutting overhead could possibly mean higher profits)? Again, if a car manufacturing plant closes, will it effect another car manufacturer that you own stock in, or is this just due to the time of year when car sales are down anyway, or rather than interpreting it to mean that people are buying fewer cars, does it just mean that the market is changing and people are buying larger cars? In other words, these articles can create a question in your mind which may be easily answered in a future issue of The Wall Street Journal. But, in the meantime, and especially while you are learning about the market, you may want to take a wait and see position. When in doubt, don't do anything. Instead look for that company that you have no doubts about.

Now if any of these businesses were on your list, what would you be able to determine? How can you use all of this research on your "gut instinct" picks to make your final beginning stock pick? What are certain prerequisites that your picks **must** have in order for you to invest in them?

If while researching your favorites, you found some of this information above, do you want to wait on that particular stock until things settle down or, because the company has such a strong history, do you want to wait for the price to drop a little because of this particular incident and buy in at a lower price? If your favorite pick is too high priced for you (or you are too impatient to save $25 a month until you have $150 to buy one share), you can continue saving or you can invest in a lower priced stock. We guarantee that you will feel very good knowing that you waited when that stock does split and you end up getting a great buy at $40 a share instead of $150. Or you can simply go to one of your other picks that has a more reasonable price of $40 a share.

There is nothing wrong with investing in your second or third pick first. If you have researched carefully and know that any of your three choices are good picks, start with the one that you can afford to start with. And if you truly cannot decide between three equally qualified stocks (we know some people have a hard time making decisions), try putting the three in a hat, close your eyes, and draw one out.

Even after your initial investment, you may want to keep an eye on The Wall Street Journal's stock quotes page. This will tell you how your particular choice is doing today. However, remember that "a watched pot never boils". It can be frustrating to watch your stock going up and down every day. For most people it is much better to look at the stock quotes perhaps once a week or at least once a month. If you are the patient type of person, the Nightly Business Report on most PBS stations is very useful both for learning more about investing and for keeping up to date on only the important things concerning your own investment. There are many other financial shows on TV but this happens to be our favorite.

The Wall Street Journal can be used for the same purpose. That is, use one of these on a daily or weekly or monthly basis (depending on how involved you want to be) to watch for important information such as when a split in your favorite stock is coming up. If you do hear or read about a forthcoming split, you might decide to quickly buy one share of that one **after it splits** to get started in your diversifying. We realize that suddenly jumping to another stock just because it drops to $40 a share is diversifying before you have collected 50 shares of your first investment. However, as you will see later in this chapter, there are very good reasons for buying just one share of a good stock at a good price while continuing to do your usual investing in your first company.

We need to point out here that all of this information can also be found online through Internet. Obviously, researching from your home is much easier, but be aware that some services do charge to enter their area. We cannot tell you in this book which ones will charge because this can and does change from week to week. But, if you have the capability, you will certainly want to check out each of your picks on Internet. If they are large enough companies (and if they are not, you should not be considering them), they will have an easy to find home page. That is, www.*name*.com. Here is where you can see their Annual and Quarterly Reports and any other information they want to give you. Notice, we said WANT to. When looking at any reports from the company, you must consider that they will only highlight the good news and try to hide the bad news from you. These large companies are usually very helpful if you send them online questions about their companies. Just remember that researching a particular company on the Internet is easy but you will not get the additional information about other companies you are interested in or any additional education in investment from the Internet. For more information and education, The Wall Street Journal will be the most useful.

You can also call any company you are interested in and ask them to mail you their most recent financial reports. To find the phone number for any business, look on that comany's Value Line page or ask your reference librarian for the phone number. Living in a free country, you can write a letter to the president or CEO of any company you want to. It could also prove interesting, and perhaps sway your choice, if you find that some executives are more willing to answer your questions than others are.

Also, if you find that you are becoming a little more interested in the stock market, our favorite daily television program is called Nightly Business Report. It is a half hour in which their aim seems to be to pack as much stock market information as is humanly possible into a half hour, so you have to listen carefully and develop a quick ear, but they do an excellent job of keeping you up to date on what is happening. And, while talking about television, if you are connected to a cable company, chances are one of your stations will have a ticker tape going across the bottom of the screen during the business day where you can watch your stock. Again, you will have to have fast eye sight to catch your particular stock. To find out what the call letters are for your stock, check the business section stock market listings of your daily paper or look beside the company name on the appropriate Value Line page.

You still have one more piece of information that you must research in order to make your money really grow. You will need to find out which companies offer automatic reinvestment plans.

3. Reinvestment. Do you have to choose only companies that have automatic reinvestment plans? No, but it is a shame to waste an easy way to make money. What is reinvestment? Every stock, if it is doing well, will have a dividend or money that it pays to you for the use of your investment money, usually quarterly. Instead of getting this very tiny dollar amount sent to you, you can choose to have it automatically reinvested in the purchase of more stock for your portfolio **without paying a brokerage fee**. That is, any dividend that you have earned is automatically used to purchase more shares of the same stock. On each quarterly statement, you will see what the dividend was and how many more shares, or what part of a share, you just got for this reinvestment. With each statement, you can watch your financial portfolio growing, even if slowly.

In order to determine whether your picks offer reinvestment of dividends, you have to do one more step in researching, but a very easy step. Again look at the bottom of the appropriate Value Line page or simply use the companies phone number and call them. We can demonstrate by using Coca-Cola as an example. Please note that it is unusual to have three splits within a 10 year period, but it is possible. The 10 year investment for Coca-Cola looks like this:

1987 buy $100 worth of Coca-Cola stock
1990 2-for-1 split
1992 2-for-1 split
1996 2-for-1 split
1997 $100 + appreciation + dividends = $1,643

So your initial purchase of $100 became $1,643 without your lifting a finger. Your investment increased 1643% or more than 16 times over a 10 year period, right? Wrong.

You also need to take into account the $25 you continued to invest every month for 10 years. By continuing to invest $25 every month in a strong company with a history of high growth that has automatic reinvestment and a good history of splits, you would end up with $100,000 in 10 years. We hope that this example will encourage you to save that $25 every single month.

Here is another interesting example. If your grandfather bought 1 share of Coca-Cola in 1919 for $40, you would now have over $191,000.00 (79 years but still very interesting). Again, this does not include investing $25 every month. However, it does include 2 world wars, 7 major depressions/recessions, and 1 major stock market crash. Is this usual for the stock market. No, there are certainly other companies that have almost as good a history as Coca-Cola does.

The reinvestment option is a simple way to make your money grow by itself. It would be foolish for the small investor to put his money into a stock that does not have reinvestment. When you get older and are looking for income from your investment, you can cancel the reinvestment portion and have the dividends sent to you. But in order to get a dividend check for $500, you need to build your financial portfolio up enough to support that kind of dividend by using your $25 each month, by reinvesting the dividends, and by picking stock that has a history of splits.

Using the reinvestment option also saves you money. If you were to go through a broker and continue buying regularly until you have 50 shares, you will be paying whatever the current price is, high or low plus paying that broker for purchasing additional shares for you. Very early in this book we mentioned the old adage, buy low and sell high. By using automatic reinvestment, you automatically buy low and sell high. As the price of your stock goes higher, your dividend will not be able to buy as much, so you automatically invest less when the price is higher. Then, when the price drops, your dividend automatically buys more stock at a lower price. And this is what everyone wants to do in the stock market - - invest more money when the market is low.

There is a second form of reinvestment to consider also.

4. Direct Cash Purchase. Before buying even one share of a company, call them to see if they have a Direct Cash Purchase Plan. This means that, after buying one share of stock, you can buy all future shares directly through the company and *they* pay the broker fees. Therefore, you are investing your money in your future and not in the stock brokers pocket. This part is what creates the huge growth for you. For instance, Coca-Cola will accept a check for as little as $10 a year. So no matter how small your budget is, you too can participate in the stock market.

5. Splits. We have been talking a great deal about splits so let's define that word. A split is when a company needs more money to invest in order to grow, i.e. upgrading of equipment or research. But the Board of Directors should only vote for a split when the value of each share is high enough to warrant it (when the stock gets "pricey"), usually when it is over $100 and the average investor can no longer afford it (remember, buy low). At that point, the company will offer a split. It can be a 2 for 1 split, a 3 for 1 split, or even a 4 for 1 split. What does this mean for you?

If a stock splits 2 for 1, it means that you bought your first share for $40 and it has now grown to be worth $80 and tomorrow you will have 2 shares worth $40 each or $80 worth of stock. Didn't make any money, did you? So why are these splits so important? Because when a stock splits, it is a very strong encouragement for others to invest (remember, buy low), and as the demand increases for this great low-priced stock, the price tends to go back up again. Therefore, in a few months, those 2 shares that were worth $40 will grow again to become 2 shares each worth $80. Your original $40 is now $80 without you spending one penny of your own money.

Now look at the Coca-Cola 10 year investment and note the splits that occurred during that time period. A company that continues to grow and split will make your financial portfolio grow quickly and easily. Your money grows without you doing anything.

How do you find out about an upcoming split? The Wall Street Journal, your local newspaper's business page, and most television news shows will announce it. Now, if you want to spend as little time as possible on your investments, do not read the next paragraph.

You see, it can be important for you to know about splits because if you suddenly come into a little extra money, immediately after that split would be the time to use it. That is, if you are getting money back from the IRS this year, or Aunt Sally always sends you a check for your birthday, or Uncle Peter died and left you everything, why not invest some or all of that extra income in your company IF the stock splits. If you are not interested in this little added bonus, then do not worry about it as your stock will continue to reinvest itself and split without you even noticing. If you do want to take advantage of the splits, you will need to spend that little bit of extra time watching the Nightly Business Report to know about it.

Another way to quickly increase your investment is to watch for the stock market to drop. A fact of life in a free society is business cycles. That is, the market will go up and down depending on who gets elected, what someone says, who died, etc. If you have a very safe stock you have invested in, and you see that stock following the rest of the market downward, and you have a little extra money, now would be a good time to buy up some more stock. Your reinvestment buys stock at the current price so that, when the price is high, it will take your reinvested dividends much longer to buy one whole share. If the market drops and your stock's price follows, you can get more stock at a much lower price. Again using our Coca-Cola example, it not only survived the 1929 stock market crash, but within two years it had gained back everything it had lost. Remember, you are investing for the long term.

What is long term? We define long term for the stock market as a minimum of 5 years but preferably 10 years.

6. This is a joke! We are adding this step just to show you what is possible. We are not recommending that you do this. We tacked to the wall one day's newspaper listing of the New York Stock Exchange. We then gave our 14 year old son, David, four darts to throw at the paper. We took the four companies that his darts hit and checked the selling price of each stock exactly one year before and the current closing price (for our purposes, we will not name them).

Stock #1 sold at 29 1/4 and closed that day at 26 3/8.
Stock #2 sold at 51 and closed that day at 58 1/4.
Stock #3 sold at 26 and closed that day at 26.
Stock #4 sold at 16 1/2 and closed that day at 14 7/8.

In other words, if he had used only this dart mcthod and bought one share of each of these stocks exactly one year ago, he would have gained a total of 2 3/4 points total for these four shares or $2.75 for the year. That does not seem like much, but the newspaper we used was during a very large two day drop in the stock market. If we waited one more week and did the same thing, his four stocks would have shown an increase of $12.11. Since he would have bought the shares for a total of $122.75, he would have had a 2% gain in one year. And keep in mind that this was during a severe correction of the market and *by throwing darts.* If we went back and showed the 10 year growth for those same four stocks, his overall gain was over 100%. This is another example of why investing for the long term rather than for only one year is more profitable. This can be a fun thing to try on paper and maybe give you a little confidence in yourself when you make informed decisions rather than throwing darts and taking your chances.

We adamantly do **not** recommend this method but wanted to show you what can happen even when you do not first learn about the stock market and research your particular investments.

V. TO MAKE THE INVESTMENT

I'm Not A Jet-Setter; How Do I Go About This Investing?

In order to invest in the stock market, you must have a licensed broker invest your money. But there is a very large difference between brokers.

In the yellow pages you will find all of your local investment brokers plus some national ones with 800 numbers. Should you use a local broker? Well, do you believe in supporting your local businesses? Do you want to deal with a live person or just a voice on the phone? You need to answer these two questions yourself. Also, you need to know that a regular broker will charge a high fee and sometimes have additional fees that they may not tell you about over the phone when you call to check out costs. Yes, you do get something for this higher fee. You will be given the brokers learned advice on your investments, and he will do the research for you, but he will not give you any guarantee that your money will grow or even that it will not decrease.

But you have to go through a broker so we always use discount brokers. A discount broker will take your order and make the purchase, period. No advice, no extra information. We believe this is the way to go because making decisions concerning your money should be your responsibility. In fact, if you decide to go with a regular broker and do as he tells you, you have taken the responsibility to make that decision and, therefore, have only yourself to blame for paying those higher fees. Our method uses only discount brokers. In return for taking responsibility and making your investment decisions, you get much lower fees.

Some nationally known discount brokers with the NYSE are First Allied Securities (1-800-448-0408, ask for Ken) or Quick & Reilly. Whoever you choose must be **listed** with the New York Stock Exchange. Please be aware that, other than FAS, brokers have a tendency to give the small investor a difficult time. Obviously, they want you to invest more and will try to talk you into any way they can.

Now let's use an average discount broker's fee of $35. This will be the amount they will charge you to make a minimum purchase. But remember that this is a one-time fee for your first purchase. After you get that first share, your dividends will reinvest without paying a brokerage fee AND each month or quarter you will directly invest that $25-a-month all without any more broker's fees. You will get your quarterly report with a form that you can send back in with your check to buy more stock directly through the company without going through your discount broker. This is why it is important to keep putting your $25 a month into your savings account.

VI. TRACKING YOUR INVESTMENTS

What If I Don't Want To Spend My Time Doing Bookkeeping?

Then don't! Tracking your investments can be fun and exciting or it can be very boring and depressing. Therefore, we suggest that you do minimal tracking but enough to satisfy Uncle Sam and enough to show you what you are accomplishing.

First, start a notebook. It can be spiral ring, 3-ring, large or small, whatever you like and will not lose. There is also specialized software you can buy to keep track of your finances on your computer. We only suggest this method if you already love using your computer and have decided you are willing to spend more time on your investments. We are going to use the notebook method to keep everything very simple for you.

In the front of the book, you will want to keep track of any stocks that interest you. When you choose one investment from the two or three possibilities you had, you do not want to just forget about the others, assuming that your research showed them to be good investments also. So keep a list of stocks that interest you with notes about any splits or how their businesses are doing.

To track the beginning stock you did choose, you will need to record the stock name, the exact date you bought it, and the exact price you bought it at. Be sure to review any brokerage fees associated with the purchase. You will be getting quarterly statements from the company so you will see the increase in value of your stock as well as any additional purchases you make through the company. Keep these reports in a folder. Your income tax preparer will need these in April. For the IRS, you will need:

1. the date of each purchase including any money invested quarterly
2. the purchase price of your beginning share and the price at the time of your quarterly purchases
3. the value your stock at the end of the year
4. any brokerage fees paid

Also, if you decided to sell any stock during the year, you will need:

1. the date of the sale
2. how many shares

3. the selling price
4. any brokerage fees paid

This is what you absolutely have to keep track of. However, if you save all of your quarterly reports, the person doing your income taxes can use those to get the necessary information. But, to make investing fun, you will still want to keep track of the gains in your purchases. Whether you do this on a daily (not suggested), monthly or yearly basis is up to you and your degree of interest.

In your notebook, you can use columns showing the increase or you can even make a graph showing monthly, quarterly or yearly changes. However, as we said before, this can be fun and exciting or it can be boring. Investing $25 a month is not a get rich quick scheme but rather a way to slowly and safely build your financial worth. The "slowly" can be boring at first, so we suggest only tracking changes once a year, perhaps right after the new year.

Your notebook might look like this:

Purchased 1 share Coca-Cola on 1/10/97 @ $42.00
Value on 12/31/97 -
6.98 per share @ $54.00 each = $376.92
Split 5/1/97, 2 for 1 -
16.12 per share @ $40.00* ea. = $644.80

*Note that the stock would not split at such a low price.

Some people may become very excited about their investments (it does resemble gambling after all) and want to track their stocks every day. This can lead to a very bad habit that is definitely not part of our philosophy. We talked earlier about letting your head rule your investments. Unfortunately, if you track every day, you may end up letting your heart take over the job. You see a sudden dip, you hear that the stock market dropped 150 points today, or you even see your stock go so high that you feel you better sell now while the selling is good. If tracking your stock too frequently causes you to make decisions using your heart, immediately change to tracking once a year and use your head.

What this all boils down to is our philosophy of investing for the long term.

Invest for the long term because, if you have chosen wisely, the market will correct itself and you will make even higher profits then you would by selling at the first sign of danger.

There will be times to **sell**. Specifically, when you have reached one of your goals such as the down payment on your new home. But even then, you do not sell immediately. Barring a terrible disaster to you or your family, you will have plenty of time to decide exactly when to sell. This time should be used to research the market again. Find out how your company is doing, is there a split coming up that you would not want to miss, has the market recently been going down and effecting the value of your stock, or has it been going up and looks like it will continue to go up? Clearly, you want to get the most for your money. So plan ahead when you need to sell some of your stock.

By the way, you will be able to sell it directly through the company but you will usually have to pay a broker fee for the sales. However, many companies have a buy-back program wherein they want to retire outstanding shares that have been issued to the public. In this case, you may be able to sell your shares back to the company without being charged any broker fees. You will want to check with the company first to see what price they will pay per share compared with the current stock market price.

VII. EASY AND SAFE INVESTING

You Don't Have To Be Rich To Become Rich

If you follow this method of investing, you will never have to spend hours worrying about your investments. By selecting large companies with a good 5 year (preferably a 10 year) track record of gains including splits, by immediately signing up for their reinvestment program, and by adding your $25 every single month, your portfolio will grow quickly. Make your money work for you instead of you working for your money.

Can you become rich on $25 a month? Well, we are firm believers that the term rich is relative. For some people, just having a retirement income of $1,000 a month will suffice. For others, only several million dollars will do. Either way, the answer to the question is yes, you can become rich on your investments. However, the best way to do that is to enlargc your investments. You may be able to afford only $5 a month right now, but what about next year? Will you get a raise and be able to make it $10 a month? What about 10 years down the road? Will you be able to afford $200 a month? All it takes is a little of your time to go over your budget each new year and decide what you want to accomplish for the coming year. And, while you are at it, look at the previous year and see if you carried through on what you wanted to accomplish. It does not matter if you did not do as well as you had hoped to do - - just start over again tomorrow.

Remember to relax and enjoy your investing. You may actually find that it is fun to become involved in what a major corporation is doing. And it is definitely fun to watch your money growing. It could even lead to a new career for you. You might even enjoy attending an annual share holders meeting. Some companies even provide their share holders with extra little perks. For instance, Hershey has been known to give out gift boxes or samples of their newest products.

A fact of life is that the only way to succeed when you start your own business is to work long hours seven days a week and never give up. Even if that business fails, figure out what went wrong and try again. In other words, there is one thing we can promise you - - you can only succeed at anything by using persistence. When you invest in the stock market, life gets easier in that you only have to persist when it comes to making that additional $25 investment each and every month.

You do not have to be a genius to accomplish what you want in life and have investments that will take care of you. You just have to spend a little time and never give up. You might decide to stop using our method and try a riskier method hoping to increase your gains. Or you might decide to just keep your money in a savings account. But whatever you do, do not give up saving for your future. If Henry Ford had given up, not only would he have poor grandchildren, but where would the economy of this country be without that transportation? You will be effecting our economy also, to a greater or lesser extent than Ford, but you will be effecting it.

The thing that people do in their lives that causes the most unhappiness is **putting it off till tomorrow**. This is true of every aspect of your life. We have written extensively about this in Bobbie's other books, but it is just as true for your financial life. You may be reading this sentence right now and thinking "next month I'll start that". Whenever you put something off, the chances of ever doing it drop dramatically. So, we want you to go get your checkbook and write a check to your bank for $25 (or whatever amount is good for you). If it is still working hours, go to your favorite bank immediately and start that savings account. If it is evening, go tomorrow as soon as the bank opens. We will *allow* you to wait until this weekend to start doing your research.

Only **you** can start building your financial portfolio (unless you suddenly inherit a great deal of money or you win the lottery). And teach your children how to invest for their future. Having the opportunity to invest your own money is a privilege that most people in this world do not have. Use this opportunity for yourself.

SPECIAL OFFER

Common Sense Portfolio Newsletter

a newsletter by the authors of
Building Your Financial Portfolio On $25 A Month (Or Less)

and

Adding To Your Financial Portfolio

By popular request, Eric and Bobbie Christensen are now providing you monthly information on the safest stock investments with the best growth potential. Each issue contains information on specific companies that has been specially picked to meet all of the investing criteria set forth in their books.

To accompany ***Building Your Financial Portfolio On $25 A Month (Or Less)***, the company chosen will have a long-term history of excellent growth and safety along with automatic reinvestment of dividends and a cash purchase plan to avoid future stock broker fees. To accompany ***Adding To Your Financial Portfolio***, a company will be chosen that has been analyzed for risk, growth potential, and timeliness for your short-term investing. You will get the specific information you need to decide for yourself.

Every monthly issue will include up-to-date information on discount brokers, current events impacting your financial decisions and other aspects of stock market investing that you need to know.

To order 12 monthly issues for $21.00
call 1-800-929-7889 (Mastercard and Visa accepted)

BIBLIOGRAPHY

Heatter, Justin. The Small Investors Guide To Large Profits In The Stock Market. Charles Scribner's Sons, NY, 1983.

Kehrer, Daniel. 12 Steps to a Worry-Free Retirement. Random House, NY, 1995.

Lehmann, Michael B. Using The Wall Street Journal. Business One Irwin, IL, 1993.

O'Neil, William J. How To Make Money In Stocks. McGraw-Hill, Inc., NY, 1995.

Porter, Sylvia. Your Finances in the 1990's. Prentice Hall Press, NY, 1990.

Quinn, Jane Bryant. Making the Most of Your Money. Simon & Schuster, NY, 1991.

Siegel, Jeremy J. and Irwin, Richard D. Stocks For The Long Run. Irwin, Inc., NY, 1994.

Spitz, William T. Get Rich Slowly. MacMillan, NY, 1992.

Walden, Gene. The 100 Best Stocks To Own In America. Longman Financial Services Publishing, 1989.

Whitaker, Leslie. The Beardstown Ladies' Common-Sense Investent Guide. Hyperion, NY, 1994.

Whitney, Russ. Building Wealth. Simon & Schuster, NY, 1994.